Shelley Lipson

IT'S BASIC

The ABCs of
Computer Programming

illustrated by Janice Stapleton

Holt, Rinehart and Winston / *New York*

Acknowledgments

I am grateful to the Ridgewood, New Jersey, elementary schools for allowing me to teach their pupils computer programming. It was the enthusiasm of these children which convinced me that young people were more than ready to learn this important skill. I would like to thank Dr. Donald Maiocco, Dr. George Libonati, and Charlotte Nash of the Ridgewood school system, for their very helpful comments and moral support.

I would also like to say a special word of praise to my friend and husband, David, who after performing surgery on his patients by day, did the same for my manuscript at night. My seven-year-old daughter, Debbie, was my first young reader whose critical suggestions I not only cherished, but incorporated in the book.

Finally, I would like to thank Miriam Chaikin, my first editor, who had the foresight to believe in this book and understand that its time had come in our society. Her sensitivity and intelligence are reflected throughout the book.

Shelley Lipson

Text copyright © 1982 by Shelley Lipson
Illustrations copyright © 1982 by Janice Stapleton
All rights reserved, including the right to reproduce
this book or portions thereof in any form.

Published by Holt, Rinehart and Winston,
383 Madison Avenue, New York, New York 10017.

Published simultaneously in Canada by Holt, Rinehart
and Winston of Canada, Limited.

Library of Congress Cataloging in Publication Data
Lipson, Shelley.   It's basic.

  Includes index.
  Summary: A simple explanation of the basics of
computer programming. 1. Electronic digital computers—
Programming—Juvenile literature. [1. Electronic digital
computers—Programming] I. Stapleton, Janice, ill. II. Title.
QA76.6.L565   001.64'2   81-20027
ISBN 0-03-061592-5   AACR2

First Edition

Printed in the United States of America
10 9 8 7 6 5 4 3 2 1

ISBN 0-03-061592-5

Contents

To my daughters
Debbie and Dana

Introduction

Computers have spread so quickly in the last few years that soon every shop, home, and office will have one. It is already old hat to play with computerized video games; computerized toasters can now *tell* you that your toast is ready; and small computers are bound to become as common to every home as the television set. Immense amounts of information, figures, and facts are available to you if you know how to push the right buttons, and everybody should learn how!

There are many kinds of computer languages, designed for different uses. This book teaches you a fun and easy computer language which lives up to its name, BASIC. The BASIC programming language was designed to be simple to use, and it has become the most popular language for the new small computers for this very reason.

But why has the computer become so important in our lives; why do millions of people need computers? We can trace the need to "mechanize information" back to the 1880 United States Census. At that time it took the Census Bureau twelve years—

until 1892—to calculate the results. This was really unacceptable since the census was taken every ten years! The 1890 census marked the first time a machine was ever used to count, sort, and do simple arithmetic with information. Thanks to this machine, it only took two and a half years to finish the 1890 census. In 1980, with the help of computers, it took only eight months to count the number of people in the United States.

Today's computer doesn't look like its predecessors, but society's need to gather and use information has grown so much that we could hardly function without data processing equipment. The computer is our workhorse. It handles huge amounts of information much faster and more effectively than ever thought possible. Our outer space programs depend on its problem-solving abilities, as do thousands of science and math labs and corporations all over the world. Doctors, store owners, teachers, students, and countless others have come to consider the computer a basic and indispensable tool.

1

What Is a Computer?

There are many different kinds of computers. They are very powerful machines. They can do arithmetic very fast and store large amounts of information.

Scientists use computers to solve complex problems. Businesses use them to keep track of their orders. And grown-ups and children use them when they play video games.

Computers are very complex machines, but they cannot think. In order to solve problems, a computer must be given a set of instructions to follow. These instructions are called a *program*. There are many different kinds of programs so computers can do many different things. There are programs which your parents can use to do their taxes. You can buy a program for a video tic-tac-toe game. Most people who use computers buy programs which someone else has written. This book will teach you how to write programs of your own.

The most common kind of computer looks like a TV screen attached to a typewriter. The typewriter is called a *keyboard*. It is used to give the computer information and ask it for answers.

When you type in these questions or answers, they appear on the part that looks like a TV screen.

The program must be inserted into the computer on a *floppy disc* or a *cassette*. Cassettes and floppy discs are permanent records of programs and you can use them over and over again. You can buy many different kinds of programs or you can learn to write your own.

```
WHICH IS THE CORRECT SPELLING?
A) CAT
B) CATT
?
```

I will type in choice "A."

Place my "X" in box number 9. I win!

```
WHERE DO YOU WANT
TO PUT YOUR "X"?
```

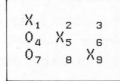

X_1 2 3
O_4 X_5 6
O_7 8 X_9

About Programming

This book is about BASIC, the language most computers understand. BASIC is a computer language invented just for students. Two professors at Dartmouth College, John Kemeny and Thomas Kurtz, developed *B*eginner's *A*ll-purpose *S*ymbolic *I*nstruction *C*ode, better known as BASIC.

BASIC instructions are easy to learn. Once you finish this book you will be able to use these instructions to write your own programs.

Before you learn the BASIC language, you should understand how to think like a programmer. The following examples are not *real* programs, but they show you how you should order instructions to write a program.

1. A program is a list of instructions in a logical sequence of steps. Each instruction is called a program statement.

2. Each line should have only one instruction. Here is a pretend program to show how to do homework. A computer would not be able to understand this "program" because it is not written in BASIC. But this is the way programmers think out problems.

1 TAKE OUT BOOKS
2 TAKE OUT PENCILS
3 READ ASSIGNMENT
4 WRITE ANSWERS

3. All program statements have *line numbers* in front of them so that the computer will know what should be done first. That means a computer reads the "program" above in the same order as the "program" below. It reads the instruction marked 1 first no matter where the number 1 appears. Every line in a computer program *must* have a line number.

2 TAKE OUT PENCILS
1 TAKE OUT BOOKS
4 WRITE ANSWERS
3 READ ASSIGNMENT

This means that if you forget an instruction you can add it at the end of your program. It's great to be able to add lines at the end—instead of typing the whole program again. Also, if you make a typing error you only have to retype the one line—not the entire program.

The best way to number the lines in your program is by 5's or 10's. This way if you make a mistake there will be room to add a line. For example, if you wanted to add the instruction "think" to our program you could do it like this:

5 TAKE OUT BOOKS
10 TAKE OUT PENCILS
15 READ ASSIGNMENT
20 WRITE ANSWERS
17 THINK

I'm beginning to see. Can we write another pretend program— one that tells the computer how to eat a candy bar?

OK, here it is:

10 BUY CANDY BAR
20 EAT CANDY
30 THROW WRAPPER IN GARBAGE

You forgot to tell the computer to unwrap the candy bar.

Right! We can just add a line at the end of the "program."

```
10 BUY CANDY BAR
20 EAT CANDY
30 THROW WRAPPER IN GARBAGE
15 UNWRAP CANDY
```

Now you have explained, in a logical order, the way to eat a candy bar. Programmers must think just like this to make a computer work.

Do you mean programs have to tell a computer each and every step, in the correct order, so that it can solve a program?

That's right. A computer does not have a brain to figure out how to eat a candy bar or do anything else. The programmer must explain how it should be done, step by step.

In a real program each line must be written according to the rules of BASIC, so that the computer will understand each step you want it to take. There are only a few instructions which you need to learn to get started. Once you understand these, the key is to use them in the right combination.

3

The Three Functions of a Computer

Every computer has a built-in electronic "brain" called a *compiler*. The compiler is like a permanent program that is made by a computer engineer. The compiler is the part of the computer which understands the BASIC language and it also knows how to do arithmetic. When you put a program into a computer, the compiler is the part of the machine that processes your answer.

When the computer is "reading" your program it is *processing*. The computer can process information much faster than you can and it is very accurate. But, a program can only be as accurate as the programmer makes it.

When you are programming a computer you don't have to think about processing—the computer does that by itself. You are interested in *input* and *output,* the two other computer functions.

If you put a cassette in your computer which you have programmed to solve math problems, you might see something like this on the screen:

```
WHAT NUMBERS DO YOU
WANT TO ADD?
?
```

If you type in the numbers 33 and 2, this is called the *input*.

The computer would now process your answer and the number 35 would appear on the screen. This is the *output*.

Here is a teacher using a computer to figure out a student's grade average. She has inserted a cassette in the computer which can do averages. She wants to average the grades 98 and 100, so she has typed in these two grades on the keyboard:

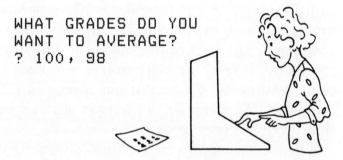

```
WHAT GRADES DO YOU
WANT TO AVERAGE?
? 100, 98
```

In less than a second, the computer processes the answer.

```
WHAT GRADES DO YOU
WANT TO AVERAGE?
```

Here's the input→ ?100, 98
Here's the output→99

Here is the same teacher waiting for the average grade of another student. But wait—she seems to be having a problem!

Yes, I am having a problem. I typed in the two test grades but the grade of 45 seems much too low. Something is wrong.

```
WHAT GRADES DO YOU
WANT TO AVERAGE?
?80, 10
45
```

In order to get the correct output you must type your input correctly. The teacher typed in the number 10 instead of 90 so she got the wrong answer. The correct answer is 85.

How does input get changed into output?

The computer processes the input and the answer is the output. The reliability of the output depends on how good the input is.

Always remember:

Good Input = Good Output
BAd Imput = sAd outpuut

4

PRINT

Let's start with an easy program which would tell the computer to print your name on the screen. If your name were Debbie, your first BASIC program would have one instruction. It would look like this:

```
10 PRINT "DEBBIE"
```

You type the line number you want to start with. Debbie chose the number 10. Then you instruct the computer what to do next by typing PRINT. You next write your name with quotation marks around it. The PRINT instruction will make the computer output any word, group of words, or numbers inside the quotation marks. The information inside quotation marks after the word PRINT will be the output. In this case the output is the name Debbie. Everything inside the quotation marks is called a *literal*.

Here is how your program looks on the screen, when you first type it in.

```
10 PRINT "DEBBIE"
```

To get the computer to output your name by itself, type in the command, RUN. The RUN command does not have a line number. It simply tells the computer to start processing. You type it at the end of your program. Then the computer knows that you have finished typing in your whole program and want the answer. Go ahead, command.

I typed RUN.

Right. Now we see three things: computer program, command, and output.

```
10 PRINT "DEBBIE"
RUN


DEBBIE
```

Here is another program which will print out a knock-knock joke.

```
10 PRINT "KNOCK KNOCK"
20 PRINT "WHO'S THERE?"
30 PRINT "BOO"
40 PRINT "BOO WHO?"
50 PRINT "DON'T CRY"
60 PRINT "YOU'RE LEARNING"
70 PRINT "HOW TO PROGRAM!"
RUN
```

When you type in the command RUN, this is what will appear on the screen:

```
10 PRINT "KNOCK KNOCK"
20 PRINT "WHO'S THERE?"
30 PRINT "BOO"
40 PRINT "BOO WHO?"
50 PRINT "DON'T CRY"
60 PRINT "YOU'RE LEARNING"
70 PRINT "HOW TO PROGRAM!"
RUN

KNOCK KNOCK
WHO'S THERE?
BOO
BOO WHO?
DON'T CRY
YOU'RE LEARNING
HOW TO PROGRAM!
```

The PRINT instruction can be used to do arithmetic by using the appropriate math sign between the numbers you are calculating.

These are some of the arithmetic operations which you can use in BASIC, along with the symbols you type in:

$$2 + 2 = 4 \quad \text{Addition}$$
$$3 - 1 = 2 \quad \text{Subtraction}$$
$$4 * 2 = 8 \quad \text{Multiplication}$$
$$6/3 = 2 \quad \text{Division}$$

Look at the screen below to see how you can program a simple math problem.

```
10 PRINT 2 + 6
RUN

8
```

As you can see, the computer output gives the answer 8. If you had typed quotation marks around 2 + 6, the computer would simply have repeated it like this:

```
10 PRINT "2 + 6"
RUN
2 + 6
```

This is because the quotation marks tell the computer to print out the literal, just like it printed the name Debbie. To get the computer to do arithmetic, simply type in your problem after the PRINT instruction, without using the quotation marks.

Here is the work of a student who did his subtraction at his desk.

$$\begin{array}{r} 67 \\ -\ \underline{60} \\ 7 \end{array}$$

And here is the result he got when he did the same problem on the computer.

```
10 PRINT "67 - 60 ="
20 PRINT 67 - 60
RUN

67 - 60 =
7
```

Line 10 printed what was written in between the quotation marks. Line 20 subtracted 60 from 67 and printed the answer 7.

This program computes part of the multiplication table for the number 5. Notice how these problems are typed so that the problem and the answer appear on the same line.

```
10 PRINT "5*1 = "; 5*1
20 PRINT "5*2 = "; 5*2
30 PRINT "5*3 = "; 5*3
40 PRINT "5*4 = "; 5*4
RUN

5*1 = 5
5*2 = 10
5*3 = 15
5*4 = 20
```

Let's take a look at line 10. When the computer read this line it first printed the literal 5*1 = as it appeared between the quotation marks. Then it printed the *answer* because the second 5*1 did *not* have quotation marks around it.

You can do addition, subtraction, multiplication, and division in one PRINT instruction. Line 20 in this next program uses subtraction and multiplication.

I wrote a program to "computerize" my shopping. I bought 3 apples at 20¢ each and a box of cereal for 85¢. If I had $2.00 to start with, how much change should I receive?

```
10 PRINT "YOUR CHANGE IS"
20 PRINT 2.00 - 3*.20 - .85
RUN

YOUR CHANGE IS
.55
```

Use a slash like this, /, to indicate division. To write 5)25 in BASIC you write 25/5 with the larger number first.

Do you understand this program?

```
10 PRINT 3/3
20 PRINT 6/3
30 PRINT 9/3
40 PRINT 12/3
50 PRINT 15/3
RUN

1
2
3
4
5
```

This program solves these problems:

$$3\overline{)3} = 1$$
$$3\overline{)6} = 2$$
$$3\overline{)9} = 3$$
$$3\overline{)12} = 4$$
$$3\overline{)15} = 5$$

5

The Arithmetic Hierarchy

This part is a little more complicated. It explains the order which must be followed to compute the different arithmetic signs ($+$, $-$, $*$, $/$) when more than one sign appears in an instruction.

What number do you think will be outputted when we RUN the following program, 20 or 16?

```
10 PRINT 4 + 6 * 2
```

The answer is 16. Are you surprised?

The reason the answer is not 20 is that the computer processes the four arithmetic operations in a specific order called the arithmetic hierarchy. Whenever a combination of signs is found in one PRINT instruction, multiplication and division are processed first, and addition and subtraction second.

1 Multiplication
  Division
  _____
2 Addition
  Subtraction

Remember, division is done before subtraction. Will this instruction output a 6 or a 1?

```
10 PRINT 10 - 8/2
```

The answer is 6. First the computer divided 8 by 2 and then it subtracted 4 from 10. The computer has completed two arithmetic operations.

When addition and subtraction or multiplication and division are found in the same instruction, the computer processes from left to right. The answer is always the same whether addition is first or subtraction is first. Look at these two problems:

$$15 + 3 - 2 = 16$$
$$3 - 2 + 15 = 16$$

It's the same with multiplication and division:

$$10 \times 4 \div 2 = 20$$
$$4 \div 2 \times 10 = 20$$

What would the result of this program be?

```
10 PRINT 15 + 3 - 2 * 7
```

Did you figure out that the answer is 4? You should have multiplied 2×7 first. Then the answer, 14, is subtracted from 15 + 3. So you got $18 - 14 = 4$.

*Is there any way
to change the order of
the operations?*

Yes, use parentheses to indicate any arithmetic function you want the computer to do first.

Here is the problem we started the chapter with, but this time the parentheses make the computer process a new problem.

```
10 PRINT "(4 + 6) * 2 = "; (4 + 6) * 2
RUN

(4 + 6) * 2 = 20
```

Notice that the way you use the parentheses changes the problem you are asking the computer to solve.

6

LET

Computers have a *memory* which is capable of storing words or numbers which can be recalled when needed. You can program the computer so that a letter which you choose, S for example, will symbolize the item you want stored. This letter, S, is called the *variable*.

Say you want to store the number 8. To do this you must type in the instruction LET as you see below:

```
10 LET S = 8
20 PRINT S
RUN

8
```

Whenever you want to output 8 in this example, you can call it out by its variable name: S.

*Is there always
a variable in the
LET instruction?*

Yes. Always put one variable followed by an equal sign after the keyword LET.

*What goes on
the other side of
the equal sign?*

You place the number you want stored in the variable on the right side of the equal sign. Actually, you can store more than just numbers using LET.

You can store letters or words in what is called a *string variable*. A string variable is indicated by a letter followed by a dollar sign, $. Place the string variable name on the left side of the equal sign and the word or message within quotation marks on the right. Here is a program that lets you store the words NEW YORK CITY in the string variable M$.

```
10  LET M$ = "NEW YORK CITY"
20  PRINT "DO YOU KNOW WHERE"
30  PRINT "THE STATUE OF"
40  PRINT "LIBERTY IS?"
50  PRINT M$
RUN

DO YOU KNOW WHERE
THE STATUE OF
LIBERTY IS?
NEW YORK CITY
```

Line 10 stores the literal, NEW YORK CITY, in the string variable M$. Lines 20, 30, and 40 print the question. Line 50 outputs the information found in M$.

Is there anything else we can put on the right side of the equal sign?

Yes. You can assign the results of any arithmetic problem to a variable. Just have the arithmetic on the right side and the answer will be saved in the variable shown on the left side. Addition, subtraction, multiplication, and division can be done with a LET instruction. The right side will look the same as it does when the PRINT instruction does arithmetic. Just use the same signs, $+$, $-$, $*$, $/$, when you need them.

This program multiplies 3 by 2 and stores the answer, 6, in R.

```
10 LET R = 3 * 2
20 PRINT R
RUN

6
```

First the numbers are multiplied. Then the answer, 6, is put into its variable, R. Line 20 then instructs the computer to output whatever is in R.

```
10 LET Q = 8/2
20 LET S = 10 - 3
30 PRINT Q; S
RUN

4  7
```

*This program
does both division
and subtraction!*

Remember that the PRINT instruction will compute your answer and output it. The LET instruction will compute your answer and store it in a variable!

*Are there rules
for making up
variable names?*

The variable name is given by the programmer. You can use:
1. Any one letter of the alphabet, A through Z
2. Any letter followed by one digit, 0 through 9

You can use S1, S2, S3, or any other letter and digit combination.

You cannot use B11, C10, or any letter followed by two digits.

And you cannot have the digit first and the letter second like these: 2E, 4V, 3D.

7

GO TO

The GO TO instruction makes the computer return
to lines it has already processed and follow the same
instructions. Look at this program:

```
10 PRINT "RED"
20 GO TO 10
RUN
```

If you run this program, the computer will print the
word "RED" over and over again . . .

```
RED
RED
RED
RED
RED
```

. . . until you push the keyboard button STOP. (**Every**
computer has a button that will make it stop. This
button may have many names. Some are called the
BREAK key. Some may have other names.)

When the program is run, the instruction on line
10 makes the computer print the word RED the first

time. The GO TO instruction on line 20 makes the computer "go to" line 10 again and it prints the word RED a second time. After this is done, the instruction on line 20 makes it "go to" line 10 again! The computer will keep on following these instructions until you push the STOP button. The GO TO instruction creates what is called a *loop*. A loop makes the computer return to lines that it has already processed.

8

INPUT

The INPUT instruction is the one that makes it possible for you to "talk" to the computer. The word INPUT is always followed by a variable. The INPUT instruction makes the computer assign numbers or words to variables, just like the LET instruction. When the computer reads the keyword, INPUT, it does these things:

1. It immediately stops processing.

2. It writes a question mark on the screen.

3. It waits for you to key in the numbers or words to be processed. These numbers or words are the input.

4. It assigns each number or word you input to the variable which follows the keyword, INPUT, in the program.

5. It continues processing.

The INPUT instruction always looks like this:

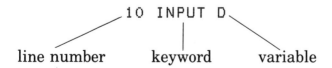

line number   keyword   variable

What has happened in this program?

```
 5 PRINT "WHAT NUMBERS DO YOU"
10 PRINT "WANT TO ADD?"
15 INPUT A, B
20 PRINT "THE ANSWER IS"; A + B
RUN


WHAT NUMBERS DO YOU
WANT TO ADD?
?17, 20
THE ANSWER IS 37
```

Lines 5 and 10 make the computer write out the message: "What numbers do you want to add?"

Line 15 makes the computer write a question mark on the screen and then wait for the user to input the numbers to be added. When the numbers are inputted, the computer puts 17 in the variable A and 20 in the variable B.

Line 20 first makes the computer write the phrase "The answer is" on the screen. Then the computer adds A and B and outputs the answer.

Hey, if I use GO TO with the INPUT instruction, I can get the computer to do my multiplication homework!

```
10 PRINT "WHAT NUMBERS DO YOU
20 PRINT "WANT TO MULTIPLY?"
30 INPUT A, B
40 PRINT "THE ANSWER IS"; A * B
50 GO TO 10
RUN

WHAT NUMBERS DO YOU
WANT TO MULTIPLY?
?24, 3
THE ANSWER IS 72
WHAT NUMBERS DO YOU
WANT TO MULTIPLY?
?19, 5
THE ANSWER IS 95
```

Here the user pressed the STOP button because there wasn't much homework!

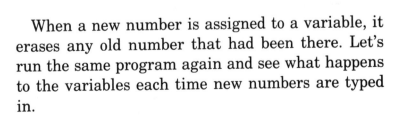

I understand that line 50 makes the computer loop back to the beginning of the program, but on line 30 the same variables are given new numbers. How can that happen?

When a new number is assigned to a variable, it erases any old number that had been there. Let's run the same program again and see what happens to the variables each time new numbers are typed in.

```
WHAT NUMBERS DO YOU ⎫          A is holding
WANT TO MULTIPLY?   ⎬ Loop 1   the number 24.
?24, 3              ⎪          B is holding
THE ANSWER IS 72    ⎭          the number 3.

WHAT NUMBERS DO YOU ⎫          A is now holding
WANT TO MULTIPLY?   ⎬ Loop 2   the number 19.
?19, 5              ⎪          B is now holding
THE ANSWER IS 95    ⎭          the number 5.
```

You can use the INPUT instruction for string variables as well.

```
10 PRINT "WHAT IS YOUR"
20 PRINT "FAVORITE FOOD?"
30 INPUT N$
40 PRINT N$; "IS MY"
50 PRINT "FAVORITE TOO!"
RUN

WHAT IS YOUR
FAVORITE FOOD?
? PIZZA
PIZZA IS MY
FAVORITE TOO!
```

Lines 10 and 20 printed the message: WHAT IS YOUR FAVORITE FOOD?

Line 30 printed the question mark. Then the computer waited for the user to type the input. The input was assigned to variable N$.

Lines 30 and 40 outputted the contents of N$, PIZZA, and the message: IS MY FAVORITE TOO!.

9

IF/THEN

The IF/THEN instruction tells the computer to compare two items and decide how to proceed with the program. It compares them by considering any one of the following questions which the programmer asks:

1. Is one number larger than the other? X>Y
2. Is one number smaller than the other? X<Y
3. Are the numbers equal? X = Y
4. Is one number larger than or equal to the other? X>=Y
5. Is one number smaller than or equal to the other? X<=Y
6. Are the numbers unequal? X<>Y

When the answer is no, processing continues to the next line, but when the answer is yes, processing goes to the line following THEN in the IF/THEN instruction.

This is easier to understand if you look at these examples:

```
10 LET M = 3
20 IF M = 12 THEN 40
30 PRINT "M DOES NOT = 12"
40 PRINT "THE END"
RUN
```

```
M DOES NOT = 12
THE END
```

Line 20 asks if the value of M is 12. Because the answer is no, processing goes to lines 30 and 40.

Let's see what happens if M does equal 12.

```
10 LET M = 12
20 IF M = 12 THEN 40
30 PRINT "M DOES NOT = 12"
40 PRINT "THE END"
RUN

THE END
```

In this case, the value of M is 12, so the computer skips line 30 and goes to line 40.

This program asks you to input the number of programs you've written today.

```
10 PRINT "HOW MANY PROGRAMS"
20 PRINT "DID YOU WRITE TODAY?"
30 INPUT B
40 IF B<2 THEN 70
50 PRINT "EXCELLENT"
60 GO TO 80
70 PRINT "THAT'S TERRIBLE!"
80 PRINT "HAPPY COMPUTING"
RUN

HOW MANY PROGRAMS
DID YOU WRITE TODAY?
? 3
EXCELLENT
HAPPY COMPUTING
```

Line 30 makes the computer ask the user for a number to be assigned to B.

Line 40 compares the value in B to 2. If the value in B is less than 2, processing goes to line 70. But the user has typed in a 3. That means the value in B is greater than 2 and processing continues to the next line.

Line 70 will not be processed whenever B has a value of 2 or more. It will only be processed when B is less than 2.

How does the IF/THEN instruction compare two values to see which is larger?

Use the "greater than" sign between the two values:

$$\text{value one} \quad > \quad \text{value two}$$

Here is a program which tells you if you are old enough to vote. To vote you must be 18 years old.

```
10 PRINT "HOW OLD ARE YOU?"
20 INPUT A
30 IF A > 17 THEN 60
40 PRINT "SORRY YOU CAN'T VOTE"
50 GO TO 10
60 PRINT "OK, YOU CAN VOTE"
RUN
```

```
HOW OLD ARE YOU?
? 15
SORRY YOU CAN'T VOTE
HOW OLD ARE YOU?
? 18
OK, YOU CAN VOTE
```

When the first student inputted the age 15, the computer went on to line 40 and printed the sentence: SORRY YOU CAN'T VOTE.

Line 50 then looped the program back to the beginning. The next student inputted his age, 18. Since his age was greater than 17, the condition on line 30 was true and processing jumped to line 60.

Did you notice that the students did not have to use the STOP key to end the loop? That's because this program ended when A was greater than 17.

In this final program, the computer will go through 3 loops and then this book will come to an end.

Here is the program:

```
10 LET H = H + 1
20 PRINT H
30 IF H = 3 THEN 50
40 GO TO 10
50 PRINT "THE END"
```

LOOP 1:

Line 10: We will use the variable H to count. When you are just starting the program the variable H is equal to zero. In line 10, you tell the computer to take the contents of H (which equals zero) and add

1. When this addition is done: $0 + 1 = 1$. The new value in H is now 1.

Line 20 outputs the value in H, 1.

Line 30 asks if the value of H is 3. Since it isn't, processing continues to line 40.

Line 40 makes the computer loop back to line 10 again, and the instructions are repeated.

LOOP 2

Line 10: In the first loop 1 was placed in H. The addition this time is $1 + 1 = 2$. The new value in H is now 2.

Line 20 outputs the value in H, 2.

Line 30 asks if the value of H is 3. Again, it isn't, so processing goes to line 40.

Line 40 loops back to line 10. The instructions are repeated again.

LOOP 3

Line 10: This time the LET instruction does this addition: $2 + 1 = 3$.

Line 20 outputs the value in H, 3.

Line 30 asks if H is equal to 3. This time the answer is yes. That makes the computer go to line 50 and output its message, THE END.

Here is a diagram of how the variable number changes when the program is run.

$$H = 0 \quad \text{before the program starts}$$
$$H = 1 \quad \text{loop 1}$$

```
H = 2   loop 2
H = 3   loop 3
```

And this is what happens when we RUN the program:

```
10 LET H = H + 1
20 PRINT H
30 IF H = 3 THEN 50
40 GO TO 10
50 PRINT "THE END"
RUN

1
2
3
THE END
```

Glossary

Arithmetic Hierarchy: The order the computer follows to process the four arithmetic operations when it has been given a PRINT or LET instruction.

BASIC: A simple computer language, invented just for students.

Compiler: The part of the computer that processes the answer.

Computer Command: This tells the computer what to do with the instructions you just typed in. RUN is a computer command.

Computer Programmer: A person who writes a list of instructions that tells a computer how to solve problems.

Data: Any kind of computer information.

GO TO: The BASIC instruction that makes the computer return to lines it has already processed.

IF/THEN: The BASIC instruction that asks the computer to make a decision. It will then go on to the next line, or skip a line, based on this decision.

INPUT: The BASIC instruction that allows the user to "talk" to the computer.

Input: Information the user gives the computer in order to receive correct answers.

Instructions: Sentence-like phrases that make up a computer program. They are written according to rules, and always contain a *keyword*.

Keyboard: The part of the computer that looks like a typewriter.

Keyword: The specific word in every instruction that tells the computer what to do.

LET: The BASIC instruction that makes the computer assign values to variables.

Literal: The message in quotation marks in a PRINT or LET instruction.

Loop: When the computer returns to instructions in a program that have already been read.

Output: The answers, or results, when the computer has finished processing the program.

PRINT: The BASIC instruction that makes the computer print out messages or the results of arithmetic problems.

Processing: What the computer does when it follows the programmer's list of instructions.

Program: The list of instructions, in a computer language, that tells the computer how to solve a problem.

RUN: A computer command telling the computer to process a program.

String Variable: The place in a computer where words and messages are temporarily saved.

Variable: A place within the computer where numbers are temporarily saved.

Index

About the Author

SHELLEY LIPSON has a long record of programming experience, first with a large corporation in White Plains, New York, and then as a free-lancer. In addition, she has taught BASIC and other computer courses at the City University of New York and at Bergen Community College in northern New Jersey. She has also taught computer programming as a volunteer to elementary school students.

Mrs. Lipson lives in Bergen County, New Jersey, with her husband, who is a plastic surgeon, and their two daughters.

About the Illustrator

JANICE STAPLETON has illustrated several books for young people. Her drawings have also appeared in the *New York Times, Fortune, Mademoiselle, Financial World,* and many other magazines. She lives and works in Manhattan.